Joel

Evolve

And

Get

Better

Every Day.

Your Friend,

Talbot Watkins III

KICKASSOPOTAMUS

Evolve And Get Better Every Day In Business And In Life

KICKASSOPOTAMUS

Evolve And Get Better Every Day In Business And In Life

CONTENTS

About TWIII

For two years in a row, *SmartCEO Magazine* ranked Talbot Watkins III as one of the top CEOs in the Baltimore, Maryland area for his work as the founder and owner of a home services company. He is also the CEO and majority owner of Titan 100, an affiliate and referral program for businesses. Born and raised in the Baltimore area, he struggled through a difficult upbringing in a home that was not really suitable for a child. He endured physical abuse, mental abuse, sexual abuse, and neglect. In his teens he tended to make a lot of poor choices, from dealing drugs to hurting people, through bouts of anger to drinking and partying too much. Talbot would pick himself up by the boot straps and become an independent young man. Buying his first home at the young age of 20 years old would be a catalyst for him to break the chains of broken generations from the past. Starting with merely $400.00 and a pickup truck at 22 years old, he would generate more than $150,000,000 million in revenue throughout his career—and it looks like he's just getting started.

Talbot is a master electrician in eight different states, a licensed real estate agent, and a licensed home improvement contractor; he has also had success in building and rehabbing real estate as well. He spent a good part of his life coaching and mentoring young men on the baseball field, and would lead his teams to high school varsity state championships. In addition, he has taken a leadership position at his church that he describes more as a servant position. He has, furthermore, delivered inspirational and motivational speeches as a keynote speaker and can often be heard from the pulpit at his church.

With only a few college credits under his belt he doesn't claim to be an academic, but he is very well read and has invested a lot of time and money into his own evolution through programs like Vistage International, Success Group, and CEO Warrior. He is courageous and would rather deliver a hurtful truth than a comforting lie; and if it's a punch in the face you need, he'll provide that free of charge.

Talbot currently is the President and Owner of Winstar Home Services. They do just about everything and anything to serve home owners, such as plumbing, electrical, heating, A/C and bathroom remodels. He is the CEO of Titan100, an affiliate program that drives business to other businesses while mentoring and coaching them. He is a speaker and author.

x

Thank You

This is the part where I guess everybody gets all sentimental and thanks the wife and kids for supporting them throughout the years. They share how blessed they are, and of course I'm also blessed and I love my family. However, I want to take time to thank the giants who have come before me. It is because I followed their examples that I am able to bless the family I so love and cherish.

People like Tony Robbins, Donald Trump, Gary Vaynerchuk and Mike Agugliaro are all Kickassopotamuses in their own right. Watching or reading how their stories unfolded has given me inspiration to do more than others.

I would also like to thank a few people who have poured into me over the years:

Susan Conord, my life coach for several years, is my friend, counselor, and role model. She has used tragedy in her own life to serve others. She helped me see through all of my brokenness. Because of the many hours I spent in her office I was finally able to see that I had value. I could see the truth about myself. Most of all, she helped heal me by teaching me to forgive. Without her help, things like this book would have never happened. Thanks, Susan.

Doug Groves, my old Vistage Chair, poured into me and helped me see the light when I thought there was only darkness ahead. Thanks, Doug,

Mike Agugliaro from CEO Warrior is one of my inspirations for writing this book. A lot of the content in which you are about to indulge can be attributed to the information I have learned through his teachings and mentoring. More importantly, he has helped me evolve faster than I ever thought possible. I am thinking and working at a level I did not even know existed. Thanks, Mike.

Brian Hamilton is and has been a good friend over the years. He has shed a few tears with me along the way; everybody needs a friend to rely on or a shoulder to cry on. Thanks, Brian.

Craig Dickerson is my director of operations and for some reason has stuck by my side through the last twenty years. Trust me when I tell you it that has been a long and hard, bumpy road along the way. His loyalty is unprecedented and it gives me real peace of mind knowing he has my back. My only regret I have with Craig is that I did not recognize his talents a lot sooner. Thanks, Craig.

Ed Gill is my accountant and, more importantly, a friend. We have bumped heads a few times over the years, but we have each come out better in the end because of it. The first time we met, he came into my office and introduced himself. I think I threw his business card in the trash before he even made it out the door. For some reason, I was led to dig it out later that day and give him a call, and boy am I glad I did! Working with him over the last couple of decades has honed my skills in accounting to the point that Ed has granted me an Honorary CPA (Certified Pain in the ASS). He has been there through thick and thin and stuck by my side. Thanks, Ed.

Of course, I do want to thank my beautiful wife, Patty. There have been many bumps in the road and troubled waters in my own evolution process. She has stuck with me through it all. I love you more each day, Patty. You make me a better man by watching and learning from you.

My sons, Matt and Nick Watkins: you are my inspiration and I love you both. You have given me a heart full of love. That love was the real game changer for me. Because of you, I would do my best to not pass down the sins of broken generations. Thanks, Matt and Nick.

What Exactly Is A "Kickassopotamus" Anyway?

What is a Kickassopotamus? Well, first off, let's just say that they are a little crazy. I mean, to go down Entrepreneur Avenue, you would have to be a little off-kilter anyway, wouldn't you? There are years of hard work, tears, and many frustrations as you head off into this so-called "glamorous" life.

Here's the thing, though: a Kickassopotamus enjoys the ride, they love the challenge, and that's not all: they kick ass. They find what

1

works and kick it into high gear on a continual basis. And even though they don't travel in herds, they are often found congregating with like-minded individuals because most people cannot relate to them. While the world runs on Ford brains, the Kickassopotamus has a Ferrari brain moving at 180 mph. They see and build things that others could never imagine. Sometimes Kickassopotamuses may seem a little on the dumb side because they think there is nothing they can't accomplish. This attribute may seem like a weakness, but it is one of their greatest strengths.

Another quality they have is they are very, very hard-headed. To date, there has never been any recording or reporting of a Kickassopotamus quitting *anything*. They are very competitive and only play to win. They work hard and are always willing to go the extra mile. They take risks, but every risk is calculated.

Most of all, they are fearless. Sometimes, when they are getting ready for a fight, they have to tie their balls to their legs just to keep them from dragging on the ground 10 feet behind themselves (I'm not sure how this works, but even lady Kickassopotamuses have giant balls). When they fight, you better not get in their way; you will get run over for sure and it will not be pretty. Even though they will fight, they love people. Sometimes their biggest battles are because they are fighting for the livelihoods of others. Kickassopotamuses don't care what others think. They say to themselves, "Why listen to the idle chatter of monkeys?" Monkeys don't create, monkeys don't do; all they do is doubt.

Kickassopotamuses are not born with the skills that take them to greatness; they evolve over time.

When it comes down to it, they love to laugh, have fun, and enjoy the ride as they travel down long, treacherous roads.

Exercise:

1. Let's write out a quick little self-evaluation of where you believe you stand on being fully evolved into a Kickassopotamus.
2. Write down five of your greatest strengths.
3. What are the obstacles standing in your way from fully evolving?

KICKASSOPOTAMUS
Keys to Success

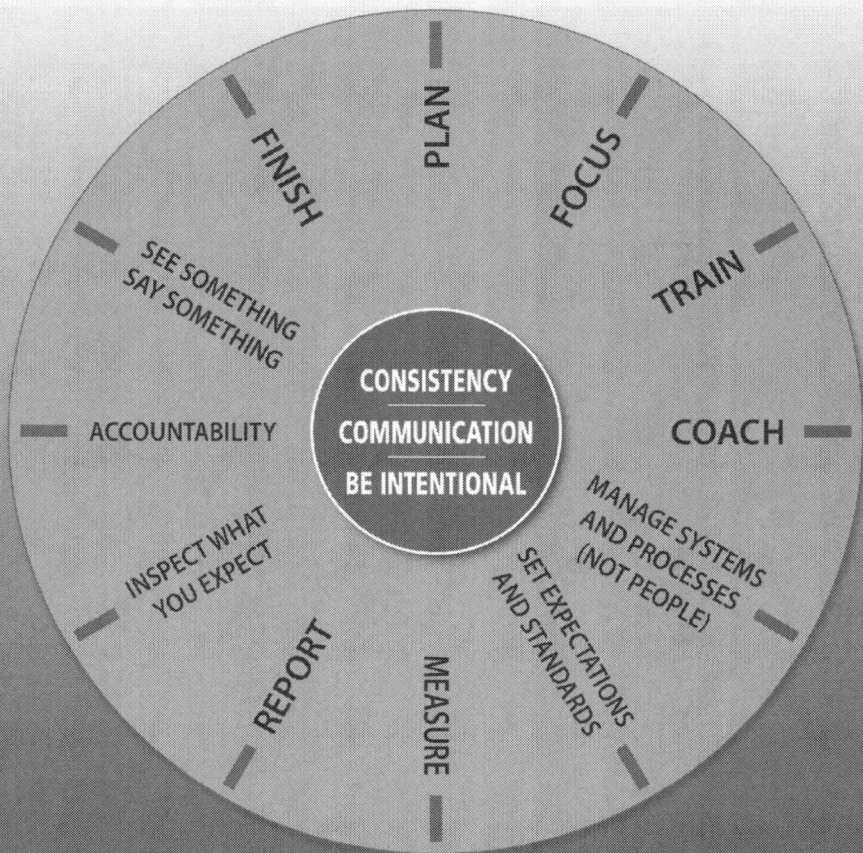

PLAN
FOCUS
TRAIN
COACH
FINISH
SEE SOMETHING SAY SOMETHING
ACCOUNTABILITY
INSPECT WHAT YOU EXPECT
REPORT
MEASURE
SET EXPECTATIONS AND STANDARDS
MANAGE SYSTEMS AND PROCESSES (NOT PEOPLE)

CONSISTENCY
COMMUNICATION
BE INTENTIONAL

The Secret Recipe To Success

I forgot to mention earlier, when I was explaining what a Kickassopotamus is, is that they are excellent cooks.

Check out this recipe for delicious Success Stew:

- 4 cups of Training
- 4 cups of Coaching
- 1 cup of Setting Targets and/or Expectations
- 3 cups of Managing (not people)
- 2 cups of Inspecting what you Expect
- 1 Cup of Measuring
- 1 Cup of Reporting

- 2 cups of Accountability
- 2 cups of See Something, Say Something

Stir with a consistent motion until the sweet smell of your world-famous Kickassopotamus Success Stew comes to a boil. Simmer, stirring with a consistent motion. Let stand, then enjoy the aroma and sweet flavors of your Success Stew.

Training

Train people. Train them some more, and then train them again and when you're done with *that* training, train them some more. Most people fail miserably at training people. It's not that they don't want to take the time or effort (okay, I'm sure some don't)— the truth is most people don't know how. The good news is, it's not that complicated. All training should be broken down into five easy steps:

1. Tell people what you want them to do.
2. Bring clarity. Tell them why you want them to do it. If the *why* is not good enough, it may be a futile task not worth the effort.
3. Tell them how to do it.
4. Show them how to do it.
5. Have them teach you the four steps above.

Repeat the five steps above until the student is a master.

Coaching

I had the privilege to coach baseball for over 20 years and I have found that there are three basic ways to coach people: 1) from the front 2) the side and 3) the rear.

- **Coaching from the front** simply means you are the HKIC (Head Kickassopotamus in Charge). You need to let people know what is expected of them. You need to let them know who plays, who sits, and who gets cut. You have to teach and train (refer to five steps of training) on a continual basis.

- **Coaching from the side** means you pour into your people on an individual basis. You find what floats their boat, what gets their engine running. I'll give you a hint here: people don't care about money, cars and fame; it's the same for everyone. They want what they think those things will give them: safety, security, respect. Most of all, people want to be appreciated and loved. Coaching from the side means you offer people a shoulder to lean on and an ear to listen. It means you lift them up in tough times and provide emotional support.

- **Coaching from the rear** means sometimes you have to get behind people and push them uphill. Don't mistake this for kicking their ass. Coaching from behind means you get in the trenches with them; it means you are willing to get dirty and work side by side with them. They need to know you are

9

there to fight for them. This was easy for me as a baseball coach. I loved to jump in the cage and show our varsity players I could still hit 90 mph fastballs (off of a machine of course); but the best thing I could do for them sometimes was fight for them. I got thrown out of a few games over the years because of a dumbass umpire making dumbass calls. This is no exaggeration.

I think every time this happened we won the game (except for once when the umpire called the game and we lost because I assaulted him. Yeah, I Earl Weavered his ass and kicked dirt on his shoes, the thin skinned son-of-a-gun! We were beating an undefeated team, too. Literally, I just kicked dirt on his shoes and that was after he threw me out. I mean, I had to get my money's worth, right?). The point is this: you have to fight for and work hard right alongside your people and have to be there to protect them.

Setting Targets and/or Expectations

It is amazing how many business owners complain about their employees and team. They complain the employees didn't do their jobs and just do the bare minimum to get by. They come in late. They don't hit deadlines. You set a process or system and it goes along great, and then a month or two down the road, you check on the system to find they stopped doing it.

Sound familiar? Insert sad face here. Most likely *you* are the problem. We say this is what we want done and this how we want it done, and sometimes we even say this is how we expect it to be done. However, we fail miserably on setting expectations. Somehow, we get caught in a game of make believe—we believe we truly set expectations. But there is a big difference. No, let me rephrase that. There is a *huge* difference. No, there is a *ginormous* difference in setting expectations and just telling people what you want done or how you want it done.

The difference is that there is always accountability when true expectations are set. You may find this hard to believe, but I would venture to say 100% of your employees want expectations set for them. Of that 100%, 95% want to be held accountable.

I honestly believe people, for the most part, are good. I am not an optimist living in fairy-land; however, I am positive that with the right culture people want to be the best they can be.

Let me give you an example of what a healthy expectation would look like:

> "Bob, out of everyone in the company, your gifts, talents, and abilities make you the most logical personal to implement the new software program."

> Now Bob knows why I chose him; more on this in the clarity section.

"My expectation is that you will have it up and running in 60 days; by the ninetieth day you will have our entire staff up to speed and trained. We'll have it up and running and fully implemented by day 120."

Here, I set dates and clear expectations.

"Bob, I really need you be a guru on this program and knock it out of the park for us."

I just reinforced the expectation.

"Please check in with me every Friday at 10:00 a.m., regardless of whether I am here, out of town, or in meetings. Always try and meet with me face to face, but if you can't, just drop me a quick email on the status of the project."

I just set up an expectation of communication.

"I will put it in my calendar to check the status with you at 11:00 a.m., just in case you get busy."

I let Bob know I will be watching.

"Bob, is this something you feel comfortable with taking on, and are the expectations fair?"

Bob says yes. Now he's taken ownership of the project.

"Bob, as you move on this project, don't let anything get in your way. When we communicate on a weekly basis, be sure to let me know if there is anything you need and I will get it for you or help you hammer something out."

I just took away opportunities for excuses.

"When we meet each week, please teach me something about the software. It's important I am in the loop and really understand it so I can share with the team how it important it is to us."

I just let Bob know he couldn't just have a fluffy meeting, but that he had to show progress and give me something substantive on a regular basis.

"Just so we are on the same page, tell me what you heard and what the expectations are."

Bob repeats back the conversation—now we are 100% clear.

"Bob, one more thing: I'll shoot you an email just outlining our meeting today, so make sure you respond so I know you got it. If you have any questions, just let me know."

Now Bob and I have a record.

We'll come back to Bob in the section on accountability.

Manage, Manage, Manage (Not People)

A true Kickassopotamus looks in the mirror often and evaluates him or herself. Usually—no, let me change that to *always*—when something fails, it is our fault, and most of the time it's because we didn't manage properly. We shouldn't try to manage people, we should manage systems and processes. A lot of failure comes from simply not taking care of the little things. I run a service company and our image is super important to me. I demand white, pressed uniform shirts with a white tee-shirt underneath; black, clean, pressed pants; black belt; and shiny black shoes with no hats. Yes, all of this is to do dirty electrical, plumbing, heating, air-conditioning, or other home maintenance work.

Prior to my days of fully evolving into a Kickassopotamus, I would get on a kick when I saw someone out of uniform and start with "That's not how we dress." Or, "That's not how we do it!" and I would get freaking pissed. Now, instead of getting emotional, I set a system in place. Every Friday my ops manager does a badge check of all our field service experts. Of course, when he is checking to make sure our guys and girls have their badges, everyone is making sure everything else is copasetic with their uniform. We take care of a minute detail and the rest of the uniform falls into place.

It may sound like we're managing people here, but we're not; we're managing ourselves through a system that is easy and scalable. *Easy and scalable* is the key here. Instead of assuming people are broken, try to find where the system has either failed or was never really set into place to begin with, then fix it and move on. The secret here is consistency. You have to continually manage all systems on a regular basis. If you don't, failure is on its way.

Measure

Measuring should be done two ways:

1. People should measure where they are along the way on a project. This just makes them aware of how far away or close they are to a target or end game.

2. The measuring should always be confirmed by another teammate or leader in the organization.

Reporting

Reporting should be done by the person who has the target or expectation set before them. It makes them self-aware, and so they will hold themselves to a higher standard than you could in most cases. Earlier I talked about managing systems. Make sure that there is a system in place that is easy and not too time-consuming to make sure reporting is done on a regular basis. Usually a five-minute weekly meeting will suffice. The key is consistency, and come hell or high water, make sure you find out where they are relative to the target.

Inspect What You Expect

Whether it's quality standards, administrative paperwork flow, or how the work actually gets done, you have to inspect what you expect. That means putting your eyes on everything. It's not that we don't trust people; it's just that we have had years of experience of doing things the *wrong way*, which has showed us how to do things the right way.

Inspections should always be done for two reasons: first, to determine whether your standards are being met; and second, to consider whether there is a better way. Inspecting what to expect also lets your people know you are truly engaged in the day-to-day business and that you care. This lifts morale when people know you care about the product or service you are delivering.

Make Them Accountable

The worst possible thing you can do is set an expectation, have people and measure and report, and then do nothing with the information. This will lead to failure almost all of the time. People actually want to know where they stand and how they are doing. For the most part they really want to know if they are meeting your standards. It gives them safety, security, respect, and appreciation. You may find this hard to believe, but most people are good and want to please you. In fact, the last thing they want to do is fail you. When they are not hitting targets or meeting expectations they want you to give them a swift kick in the ass. It shows you care enough to discipline.

Some ways to hold people accountable:
- o Let them know exactly where they stand.
- o When failing, go back to step two of training: bring clarity and deliver the why.
- o Let them know the consequence of their failure for the company and themselves.

- o If need be, share the four steps of discipline (no worries, it hardly ever gets to this point but it is necessary sometimes):
    1. Verbal documented warning
    2. Written warning
    3. Written warning with a week off, as well as a meeting to discuss if they are a good fit for the company
    4. Termination (don't worry, you didn't fire them, a true Kickassopotamus understands we never fire people, they fire themselves)

The very best ways to hold people accountable:
- o Celebrate their victories
- o Celebrate hard work
- o Share their victories with everyone
- o A special touch, a nice letter home to their family thanking them for sharing their loved one with you and letting them know the impact they made for you. Deliver the why again.

Remember Bob's Project? If the project does not make the deadline, most likely it's your fault. We get busy, we don't follow through, and we start to miss the meeting for whatever reason. We use the old "Bob has it handled" excuse. We delegated and it's off our plate. You freaking dumbass, you just took all the wind out of Bob's sails. Now you are two months down the road and wondering why in the hell Bob only has a few things done on the project. Now you want to wring Bob's freaking neck. The truth is you never held Bob accountable. The meeting or weekly follow-up literally would have taken a whole 10 minutes out of your day, but other things were more important (maybe you should get off of Facebook for that 10 minutes).

Let's play this another way. You are striving to become a Kickassopotamus and have followed through with the meetings, and now Bob missed a meeting. You don't let it slide. Let me teach you something that Mike Agugliaro from CEO Warrior and Gold Medal Services taught me: **The Four Steps of Discipline.**

> Me: "Bob, we agreed you were going to meet with me every week and give me updates and teach me something on the software, didn't we?"

> Bob: "Yes." (Bob just took ownership of the failure. If you held up your end don't accept excuses.)

> Me: "Bob, didn't I explain how important it was that we get this done?"

> Bob: "Yes." (We just reinforced the expectation.)

Me: "Bob, I set the expectation; I was super clear, and you repeated it back to me. You took ownership of the project."

"Bob, I have to give you a documented verbal warning here. All that means is I will drop a note in your file so I have it on record in case we have to deal with this issue in the future. Just make sure we move forward and this never happens again. Bob, whenever we have a situation like this we feel we owe it to our team to run through the four steps of discipline. Let me run through them with you real quick."

I then explain to Bob the discipline policy below:
"The *first violation* is a verbal documented warning. That just means, hey, we had a quick conversation and I explained the problem or failure with you and I put a note in your file. I walk you through the four steps of discipline. After that we moved on like it never happened.

"The *second violation* is written warning. I put a notice in writing and we have you sign it. I explain the problem again and I walk you through the four steps of discipline. After a year it comes off your record.

"The *third violation* is exactly the same as the second violation; however, this comes with a full week suspension without pay and you cannot use vacation time to cover it. After returning we will sit down together and decide if you are a good fit.

"The *fourth violation* is termination. At this point we feel as though the employee took themselves out of the game and walked off the field and we just make it official.

"Are we clear, Bob?"

Bob: "Yes."

Me: "Okay, great. Let's put this behind you and I look forward to hearing from you next week."

Regardless of the expectation, the system will work. The key is consistency. If you have a uniform policy and the expectation is that the shirt will be tucked in, that means it is tucked in at all times when he is on the clock. The first time you walk by and do not address it, the expectation is worthless. Remember, common sense should always come into play. Simple reminders are okay without documented verbal warnings, but be careful that you are not saying the same thing over and over to the same person.

You cannot play the game without an end in mind. People actually want to know what is expected of them. We were built to compete and play. You can spend all the time in the world coaching and training, but if you don't set targets there is nothing to shoot for. Setting targets, goals and expectations actually energizes people.

Here is a little secret: exhaustion hardly ever comes from working hard, but rather exhaustion comes from boredom. Not having targets makes the work at hand futile at best. Set targets and watch your people go.

See Something, Say Something

How many times do you or a key manager walk by something that is not up to your standards and you simply say nothing? It is easy to stick your head in the sand and do nothing. Seeing something and not saying something is often a result of avoiding confrontation, or you use the excuse that you don't want to hurt someone's feelings, or (and this is a scary one) you are just lazy and it will cause more work for you and others or your team.

The problem with seeing something and not saying something is that every time you fail to do so you lower the bar for yourself and everyone on your team. It means you are willing to accept mediocrity. Worst yet, the people on your team who follow the rules and see you avoid or turn a blind eye to following your own systems, processes, and procedures will have contempt for the person getting special treatment; eventually, that contempt will be directed at you. Remember: as leaders, it's our job to bring people up to a level they never even knew existed. When you avoid having a courageous conversation with someone, you are essentially telling them, without saying a word, that they are not worth your time or effort.

> **dis· dain**
> dis´dān/:
> *noun*: the feeling that someone or something is unworthy of one's consideration or respect; contempt
> *verb*: Considered to be unworthy of one's consideration

The Secret Sauce: Consistency

- o Consistency
- o Be consistent
- o Consistently repeat and train, coach, set targets and expectations, inspect what you expect, measure, report, and hold people accountable.
- o One more thing: Be consistent

Setting Standards

We talked about expectations and setting targets for the business. It is just as important to set expectations and targets for yourself. The problem is setting a target and not knowing how *who you are* could lead to failure as a parent, spouse, leader, and business owner. Not knowing who you are may be the reason you are fat, out of shape, or you smoke like a chimney, even though you have made a New Year's resolution for the past twenty years to lose the weight, get in shape, or quit smoking. Most people use the excuse of willpower, stress, or a busy life to fail at the targets they set for themselves. People are, for the most part, born with an incredible amount of power; the sad fact is that 99% of people never harness it. The truth is, outside of mental illness, if someone decides to do something, they can accomplish it. The greatest achievements in life almost always happen on purpose.

I have strong political views, but I never talk politics. This is because usually there is nothing to gain by it. However, I will take my chances. If you are reading this book there is great chance you think like me anyway and will not be offended. Here it goes: socialism *never* works. Redistributing wealth from the rich and giving to the poor has never worked any time in any country. If you took all the wealth from the top 1% in the world and gave it to the poor, in a very short time the top 1% would be back on top.

A perfect example: the lottery. Many people who win the lottery find themselves broke and destitute in a short amount of time. Unfortunately, there is story after story of lottery winners who have lost it all in a short period of time. You can give excuses as to why this happens, things like, "Well, they were never taught how to handle money." I would say that statement is true for the most part, but it is not the biggest problem.

On the flip side, how many stories have you heard about top performers failing miserably, and in a year or two they are on the cover of *Forbes*?

Don't think for a minute that the people who fought their way back to the top somehow got lucky (I might have to reach through this book and punch you in the face). They did it through hard work and perseverance. The point is that they set standards for themselves and live by their standards. I am not talking about expectations, I am talking about standards. Successful people have a standard for themselves that always exceeds what the common folk set for themselves. Successful people outwork, outperform, and out think others, because that is their standard.

Your standard will always determine who you are and where you go in life. Most people aren't fat because they are "big boned" or inherited the condition from their family. They are fat because they have no standard of diet or health for themselves.

I have fought the battle of the bulge myself over the years, so I am speaking as an expert. Until I made being healthy a standard, I stayed a fatass. Think of an athlete. Their standard is a tight, toned, and strong body. Because they have that standard, they eat healthy and work out hard six to seven days a week.

The point: your standards determine who you really are. If your standard is to work hard at academics, almost by default you become the A-student and it doesn't even seem that difficult. Set a standard and be that person. Tony Robbins talks about this often when he says, "People say I should do this, I should do that; basically they should all over themselves." He goes on to say, "Turn your 'shoulds' into 'must.'" The easiest way to do this is set standards and be that person.

What are the musts in your business? The best way to say, "This is who my business is"? Give it a personality.

More importantly: what are your standards for yourself?

Answer these questions:

1. Who am I?
2. What kind of father or mother am I?
   a. What does that mean?
   b. What is my standard?
3. What kind of husband or wife am I?
   a. What does that mean?
   b. What is my standard?
4. What kind of leader am I?
   a. What does that mean?
   b. What is my standard?
5. What kind of entrepreneur am I?
   a. What does that mean?
   b. What is my standard?

Dig deep. Add anything to the list that you need to set a standard for, and become that person. Yes, it will still take time and hard work, but it is worth it.

Example:

a. *What is my standard of personal health?* My standard of heath is that my weight is controlled and I maintain a healthy weight.

b. I will always weigh under 220 pounds. (Give me a break, people, I am big boned.) (Okay, fine, I carry a lot of muscle weight.)

c. I keep my heart and body in shape through regular cardio workouts.

d. I constantly become stronger through lifting weights.

Accountants Suck

Accountants suck. Yes, you heard me right, accountants suck. Sorry, Ed. Ed is my accountant and good friend and I value his services. More importantly, I value his friendship. Having said that, he still sucks.

Accountants are, for the most part, analytical. The problem with analytics is that, in order to be analytical, you have to have data to analyze, which means most accountants get stuck in the rut of reviewing historical data. They are too busy making sure all the debits and credits are put on the correct line of the income statement and balance sheets. They can't help it; they went through four years of university and then they most likely went on to two to three more years earning their masters in accounting with an emphasis on one aspect of accounting, such as a specialization in taxes. Their college years are focused on the accuracy of data, making sure all the journal entries are coded correctly, and making sure depreciation is added to the income statement to cover interest. They cover the principal part of the payment that is not deductible except through depreciation. Even worse, they spend every year talking about ethics. Of course, ethics are important; however, professors turn ethics into protection. They spend tons of time on what not to do and how not to get sued. A lot of their professors either have failed in the real world or never actually lived in it and run a successful business. As a result, they get into the academic world and pass on their fears as if they are doing a great justice and service to the world.

At the end of the year, accountants will get a really good feeling about themselves because the government will extend section 179 and allow you to deduct entire large purchases from your bottom line. They stick their chests out and say something like, "I just saved you a ton of money by letting my clients know about this fabulous thing called section 179, and now my client can run out, make a purchase, and finance it over the next five to ten years with no deductions available after year one. If you make a purchase strictly for the purpose of saving taxes, it is probably a pretty dumb move."

The year is over and the numbers are in and you barely broke even. I would normally say you have no one to blame but yourself; however, the so-called professional accountant that you paid thousands of dollars to could really have helped make a difference in your financial life. He had the numbers at his fingertips on a regular basis and he did nothing with it. He made no recommendations. After all, why would he? He might get sued. He can take great pride, though, in knowing that everything is perfect on the statements and if an audit comes you are protected. BFD. (Let's say that stands for "big freaking deal.") Even if you do get audited, chances are the sting would be limited because you made no money, just like the other 95% of businesses in the world.

If I were an accountant (and thank God I am not) I would measure my level of success by how many of my clients were truly successful and had healthy businesses. Even more importantly, I would look at the effect I had on improving their bottom line. I would take great pride in knowing how I helped improve their current ratio and quick ratio. How did I help improve the equity on the bottom of the balance sheet? How did I affect their lives personally? I would ask myself if I helped my clients grow their personal wealth. Instead, accountants like to brag on the hours they put in during tax season and how many returns they completed. The over-educated dumbasses (Sorry, Ed, I still love ya) could work half the hours they put in and serve 75% fewer clients just by helping businesses be successful. If they built that kind of value they could charge two to three times more money and no business owner in the world would even blink an eye at the cost.

I had the opportunity to listen to Mike Michalowicz speak at a very small and intimate event. Mike is the author of the book *Profit First*.

His book is both brilliant and simple. It is worth the read and I highly recommend it.

In it, he explains that the GAAP method of accounting is a real recipe for disaster and failure. He explains the old formula of:

$$Sales - Expenses = Profits$$

This formula just doesn't work. I will do him the honor of not getting into why and hopefully let him explain it for himself when you purchase and read his book for yourself.

This is his alternative:

$$Sales - Profits = Expenses$$

It seems too simple, but this formula is a real game changer.

Using this formula, I created a simple spreadsheet, in which I counted profit as the first expense. That is where the work begins. If you got into business for any other reason than to make a profit, get the hell out right now because you are screwing up the market for everybody else. You suck. Yes, you can serve people and charities and make a difference in the world, but if you're not profitable, how can you serve?

Let me circle back around to listening to Mike speak. He shared that he received a call from an accounting organization with thousands of accountants in it; they wanted him to be the keynote speaker at an event. He was excited to get his story out and have an opportunity to serve other business owners by teaching these accountants his simple formula for making money. Here is the unbelievable kicker—and I am absolutely positive this is exactly the way it went down. After Mike shared his ideas, formula, and story, the group disinvited him. He didn't fit their mold, their years of doing the same thing over and over with the same results, the same goal ("don't get sued").

$$Sales - Profits = Expenses$$

It is freaking brilliant. I am not trying to sugarcoat it. If you really strive to become a Kickassopotamus this is where the hardest work and the toughest decisions have to begin and be made on a regular basis. After a short time in business it becomes pretty easy to project sales month-over-month; then it's time to look at cost and make sure you're in it to win it. Make sure you don't use any excuse not to make money. Not growth, not the market, not the competition. Figure out quickly what is working and what is not and adjust accordingly.

Here is the bad news. You're in business, you're striving to be the most successful Kickassopotamus on the planet and with that goal and title the tough decisions are yours to make. Here is the worst news: if your accountant was worth his weight in salt he would say, "Hey, your fixed costs are a little high but they're manageable. The problem is that your direct labor and overhead labor are way out of whack and until you make cuts you are never going to be successful. Unless your hands are tied with a huge mortgage and sales are down I would say 99% of all money is lost in the managing of labor."

Just to clear something up: don't use the mortgage or dropped sales as an excuse to fail either. Most business owners are more passionate and care more about people than the average Joe and this can be a real business killer. This is because we are not cutting labor but we are cutting people. Here is your choice: cut the people, or close the business. And do yourself a favor: if you can't cut the people, close your doors immediately. I mean, why put in all the hard work if at the end of the day your heart won't allow you to follow the wisdom of your mind and gut? And at the end of it, you and all your employees are going to have to get jobs somewhere else anyway? Give them and yourself the opportunity to start new careers so they can get on with life. After all, you probably never really had what it took to be a Kickassopotamus.

Back to the accountants. Data is data and it can be valuable, but it doesn't tell you the next big product or service you can provide. Data doesn't manage labor and control cost. You do! Be sure when hiring an accountant you find one with a track record of successful clients, and that, even more importantly, he or she has had the balls to fire the ones who wouldn't move and manage their businesses to profitability above the industry standards.

Finally, as I end this chapter, let me say this: make sure you get a CPA and not some bookkeeper who learned how to use QuickBooks and now professes to be an expert on taxes and accounting. The few dollars you save paying the untrained bookkeeper could end up costing you big dollars in taxes. You get what you pay for. And, after all, you're going to be extremely profitable now. God forbid you ever get audited by Uncle Sam; if you do, you do not want to walk in there without a CPA. They will eat you up and spit you out.

There, Ed. I hope that made you happy and that we can still be friends.

Patriot Electric Inc. Profits Budgeted First		
		Feb-16
Operating Income	Monthly	
Income	745,000	100.00%
Profit Budget	74500	10.00%
Direct Expense		
Material	310,000	41.61%
Equipment Expenses		0.00%
Subcontracted	19,000	2.55%
Other Job Expense		0.00%
Direct Labor w Burden	165,000	22.15%
Superintendant Labor w Burden	30,950	4.15%
Small Tools/permits	7,500	1.01%
Cost Of Goods Sold	532,450	71.47%
GROSS PROFIT	212,550	28.53%
Remaining Budget To spend on G&A EXP.	138,050	
General Admin Exp and OH	135,000	18.12%
Over Under Profit Budget	3,050	Under Budget - Mission Accomplished
Total Net Profit	77,550	10.41%

Part 1 of Profits Budgeted First spreadsheet. Go to
www.kickassopotamus.com to get a copy of this spreadsheet.

General Admin Exp and OH		
Equip/Shop Expense		
Shop Labor		
Equipment Lease Expense		
Equipment Fuel		
Equipment Supplies & Maint		
Equipment Repair		
Rent		
Office Supplies		
Utilities		
Telephone		
Cellular Phone		
Internet & Web		
Office Equipment		
Computer Expense		
Bank Charges		
Postage & Freight		
Janitorial		
Advertising & Promotion		
Accounting Fees		
Legal Fees		
Legal		
Travel, Meals, Entertainment		
Car Allowance		
Allowance		
Dues & Subscriptions		
Continuing Education		
Emp Varification Expense		
Uniform Expense		
Charity Donations		
Office Maint & Repair		
Medical Expenses		
General Insurance		
Taxes & Licenses		
Interest Expense		
Bad Debt Expense		
Plan Fees		
Bonding Fees		
Overhead Labor W Burden		
Officers Salaries w Burden		
Vehicle Maint/Repairs		
Vehicle Fees		
Fuel		0.00%
Tolls & Parking		
Vehicle Lease Expense		
Navtrak Expense		
Vehicle Traffic Fines		
Small Tools		
Shop Supplies		
Vehicle Depreciation Expense		
Total G&A	135000	

Part 2 of Profits Budgeted First spreadsheet.

Go to www.kickassopotamus.com to get a copy of this spreadsheet.

Action and Purpose

Action without massive purpose will rob you of your fortune, time and life. I will talk later about finding your purpose in life. There is another kind of purpose that is super important as well: the purpose of what you are working on at any given moment. Yes, everything needs to revolve around your business and personal purpose statements (some people call these mission statements, but not me). However, I am talking about the individual task at hand.

I once had an employee who was the first one to work every day, and I mean every day. He was also usually the last one to leave. He worked harder and longer than most people. He spent most of each day putting out fires. His results were often poor and it brought down other parts of the company and team. People would get frustrated and make little digs and try to get in my head to help me see the light. I knew he was failing and spent years hoping he would become better. It never happened. His hard work never paid off for the company. It only disproves the old adage "Hard work beats talent when talent doesn't work hard."

In the end I would come to see the light; I was in a hole, so he was terminated. People immediately came to me and said, "Thank goodness; what took you so long?" It came down to the fact that I couldn't see past his hard work and effort. The man even outworked me as the owner of the business (No worries; that was before my evolution into a Kickassopotamus.) He also was not afraid to hold people accountable and I loved that. I often wonder whether, if I had the opportunity to mentor him today, it would produce the same result.

Yes, success takes hard work. However, it takes hard work plus purpose. It also takes complete focus on the task at hand. Another quote I am no longer fond of is, "Work smart, not hard." I am sure it has been said before, but I have never heard it so I will claim it for myself, "Work hard AND smart."

Ask yourself these questions when working on a task:

- Is what I'm doing right now going to move the needle?
- Will it make money or improve my life?
- Will it move me closer to my targets?
- Will it bring profits or build my personal wealth?
- Does it fit my purpose statement (mission statement)?
- What is the next action?

Getting Lost

I had an opportunity to hear a friend of mine, Rob Roell, speak about the art of getting lost, of getting outside your comfort zone. He shared about the guitar solo that Eric Clapton played with Cream at Winterland, about Robert Johnson's song *Crossroads*. If you haven't heard it, stop reading and go give it a listen. It is truly amazing.

In an interview, Clapton was asked about the solo. The reporter said to Clapton, "As of today, that solo is still considered one of top solos of all time." He prompted Clapton to give his insight on the event and his own creativity. Clapton laughed and explained that actually it was a hectic day, and that things were a little crazy and that he got lost in the moment. He was lost in the moment and managed to create one of the greatest pieces of art of all time.

Rob's point was simple: when you let yourself get lost in the moment, you can create some of your best work. In order for this to happen you truly have to find your passion and purpose. Finding these will allow you to get so deep into your work that it just happens. You will create and do things you never imagined were possible. I can tell you from my own experience it actually comes easily when this happens. On the other hand, getting lost without a plan to find your way out of the forest is an entirely different story.

Years ago, before I found my own passion, purpose, and power, I would spend time doing things like hunting, fishing, and spending time at the bar. Twice it would happen that on a hunting trip I would get lost. When I say lost, I mean *lost* (don't laugh, it's easy to do and this was before GPS was in everybody's hand via their smartphone). The first time I was kind of lucky because I was in a small mountain area in the Shenandoah National Park. I just started walking downhill and eventually came to a road that led me to safety.

The second time I got lost was a different story altogether. I left my stand and started to track a nice white-tailed buck. Before I knew it, I got turned around and lost sight of my stand. I started walking, looking and looking for my stand. I even walked in what I thought were circles, so I was positive I would have to come up on it eventually. Of course, that never happened. I was in a totally flat area and everything looked the same. When I say everything, I mean *everything*. Every tree, every bush, and every weed looked the same. I thought, "Well, I'll just keep going, and just like last time I'll find a road and that will lead me home."

So off I went. Time passed and it was starting to get dark. To say the least, a little worry and anxiety set in. I was beginning to think about hunkering down for the night and finding a place to sleep. I was worried about what my wife would think when I didn't make it home for the night; I didn't want my dumbass mistake to cause her worry and anxiety. With these new thoughts, I was motivated to keep going. I passed a pond and was happy that it looked different than everything else I had seen over the past hour. I thought this was a good sign, so onward I pressed.

Sometime later I would cross what looked like someone's private property, as there was a field in the middle of the woods. I searched the surrounding area for a home of some type, to no avail. I started to lose hope again. Nevertheless, I went on, and soon I found myself crossing over railroad tracks. Why in the hell were there freaking railroad tracks in the middle of the woods? I had to be close to some type of civilization, but in actuality it was just another tease that would lead to desperation. It's not warm outside during hunting season by any means, so I had to brave the cold and whatever other elements old Mother Nature had to throw at me for the night. I had just lost about all hope.

All of a sudden I noticed an opening in the trees a few hundred yards away. To say I got excited would be an understatement. After a few hours of walking I gained new energy and started to get a little gallop going toward the end of the tree line. This was it; I was getting out of those freaking woods and I would not have to worry about what my wife was thinking at home.

As I neared the end of the tree line, I could hear what I thought was wind in the clearing. All I had to do was scale the first hill I had seen for hours and I would be on the other side to freedom. But as soon as I got to the top, my heart sank. The wind I heard was actually waves crashing against the shore. I was now standing on the banks of the western shore of the Chesapeake Bay. The entire time I had been headed east, when I should have been going west. All I could do was sit there and catch my breath. I tore myself a new one: "Talbot, you are a freaking dumbass."

After a few minutes of kicking my own ass, I calmed down. I had to make a real decision as to whether to spend the night or walk west. The good news is that I knew exactly where I was, because I had spent quite a bit of time on the Chesapeake and things were familiar to me. The only option was to go back the same way I had come. After knowing where I was, finding my way out was easy. I just had to make sure I headed west and did not get distracted.

One thing I am sure of is that if I had taken a compass in the woods with me and had obtained a reading of where I was before I went in, I would have easily found my way out. To this day, I wonder what would have happened if I had stopped walking for a while, if I had tried to get some bearings and come up with a plan of action to find my way out. My gut tells me I would have spent a lot less time lost.

That's a long story, but the lessons I learned from it are still valuable to me to this day. You need to know where you are at any point and time in life. You have to self-assess (be honest) and come up with a plan (a map, if you will, of the direction you want to go). Here is the coolest thing about creating your map: you do not have to follow anyone else's map. You have the ability to cast vision, set targets and goals that are your own and no one else's. When creating your map, it is crucial that you know exactly where you are. In order to do that, you have to stop, look at your surroundings, and figure out what is working and not working in your life. That is the first step to finding your path to success. When creating your map you have to be intentional, set targets, and establish a plan that will lead to freedom, and then finish what you started.

It's simple: **Plan. Focus. Finish.**

As you are an ever evolving Kickassopotamus stop for a moment and answer these questions:

1. Where am I right now in my life?

2. What is my passion?

3. What is my purpose?

4. What can I see that no one else sees (be selfish here, it's your map)?

5. Where do I want to go? (What's the target?)

6. What is the "Why"? (If the why is not strong enough, you may not have enough passion to succeed.)

7. What are my current skills and abilities?

8. What skills do I need to hone to evolve?

- What's working and what's not?

9. What am I going to *stop* doing? Why? When? (In other words, what's not working?)

10. What am I going to *start* doing? Why? When? (What are you not doing that you know is creating failure, and by not doing it will reap rewards?)

11. What am I going to *keep* going doing? Why? (What's working?)

12. Remind myself of the target and ask: What is the next action step I need to take?

13. What is the next action step?

14. What is the next action step?

15. What is the next action step? (Get the point?)

16. Finish

Vision Is <u>Not</u> The Most Important Thing

The greatest men and women of the world were true visionaries. They could see things others could not even imagine. Names like Edison, Franklin, Einstein and Jobs come to mind pretty quickly. This is true of the Kickassopotamus.

Take an empty piece of land, for instance. One person simply sees it for what it is: a nice wooded area. Another thinks it would be a nice place for a park. Another person thinks it would make a great little housing community; then someone else steps up and sees a hospital to serve and care for people in the community. The next thing you know, the man with the greatest passion to serve the community steps out in faith and gets things moving, and voila! There's a new hospital in that little old piece of wooded land.

The point is this: every great idea, every venture, every invention started from the beginning of time has started in the mind of one man. Great businesspeople get a gut feeling, and the greater the stomach churns the greater the passion becomes. Then action starts to happen and things come to life.

Don't mistake an idea for a vision. I know all the so-called gurus out there in the business world are screaming from the top of mountains, "You must have vision, you have to have vision, you absolutely have to have vision!" You have to be really careful here not to focus so much on the vision, as you will forget about the product or service you are offering.

Business owners learn a little when they start to have some success, and they forget what got them there. Let's say they start with a nice little plumbing company, and they do an amazing job for their clients. The next thing you know, they have to add a few employees, and then a few more. Before you know it, the tool belt comes off and they consider themselves super CEOs. They start working and spending time on building mission statements, setting visions and goals; they nail down their core values…and at the end of the day, they forget what got them successful in the first place. It wasn't vision, goal setting, mission statements, or core values. It was providing great service one customer at a time.

Kickassopotamuses understand if you sell plumbing, you have to provide great service and do it again and then do it again and then do it again. Setting short-term targets while staying focused on the thing that you actually provide—doing an amazing job serving your customers—will reap you greater rewards than spending too much time on an unknown future.

Exercise:
1. What do you see that no one else sees? It can be anything.
2. Is it worth pursuing?
3. Set a target.
4. What's the next action toward your target?

Play To Win Or Don't Play At All

Take time and read George Cloutier's book, *Profits Aren't Everything, They're the Only Thing*.

His book is hard-hitting and tough. It takes guts to get through it, but do it. His whole premise is to not be a fool, do the work, make smart decisions, and reap the rewards.

In sports there is a score board; in school there is a report card; in games the first one to the finish line or the person who dominates and takes everything away from everyone else wins. Therefore, the measuring stick to see who the winner is usually pretty easy.

In business one might think it's the balance sheet or income statement that decides if you are a winner or loser. Be careful to not get caught in that trap. Depending on the type of business you are in, a great balance sheet could be the wolf in a sheep's clothing. Assets could outweigh liabilities 5 to 1 (that would be your current ratio), but at the end of the day if it's all tied up in A/R or working process you could be headed for real trouble. Your score card should be your bank account. You should review your bank account month after month and determine whether the balances grew, and if they didn't there is a problem. Of course it can't grow from holding on to unpaid bills, so you should make comparisons month to month and make sure the A/P didn't grow and your ratios improved. However, the real score is cash on hand. Did your personal wealth grow as well? These factors are the real scorecard that tells you whether you are winning or losing.

In high school my favorite sport was wrestling. There was nothing like it. It was you and your opponent on that mat *mano y mano*. One-on-one with no one there to back you up. You either lived or died on your own accord. Sure, they kept a team score but what the hell did I care if my team won or not? Often my team would lose and I would be headed home a winner with my head held up high. I was kind of a peacock on the ride home. Dan Gables, who a lot of people regard as the greatest wrestling coach of all time, said, "Gold Medals are not made of gold, they are made of hard work, determination and hard-to-find alloy called guts." Those three characteristics are truly a key to success.

- There is no substitute for hard work, and the old cliché that you should work smart rather than hard is a huge fallacy told by lazy people. The fact of the matter is you need to work smart *and* hard. Talent can take you far but the old saying that "hard work beats talent when talent doesn't work hard" for the most part is true. You have to be willing to get dirty, roll up your sleeves, and do whatever it takes to win.

- Another word for determination is "perseverance." The question is not *if* you will get knocked down, the question is: *when* will you get knocked down. It's coming and it's going to happen on more than one occasion. You have to have fortitude to fight; you have to be willing to get back up dust and yourself off and put yourself back in the game. I love it when Rocky said, "It's not how hard you can hit, it's how hard you can be hit and get back up and keep fighting." We already decided that a Kickassopotamus never quits, but on the off chance you have to mentor or coach someone without the Kickassopotamus DNA, remind them that pain is temporary and it may last a day, a week or a year; but eventually it will leave the body. However, quitting—*quitting is forever.*

I want to stop here for a second and share something with you. It will piss off a few people I have had the misfortune of not being able to pay back what I owed them in full.

Sometimes you have to start over, or do a reset, if you will. This is not the same as quitting. Things happen and sometimes they are out of your control; other times. you just made some really poor choices. It's not the first century, where you are put into indentured servitude or thrown into prison for perhaps the rest of your life. It's why bankruptcy laws were passed; sometimes it's the only option. Don't take it lightly and really consider all of your options before you decide to start over. There are a ton of things to think about and you have to have a tough resolve to go through a Chapter 11 or 7. But if there is no light at the end of the tunnel it may be the only action for you that makes sense.

I'll share this with you: one of my key suppliers, who I thought was the only game in town, was furious with me because I had to make the decision to start over. I had my bank breathing down my neck and they were calling a 3-million dollar balloon due. Five years of never missing a payment at 25k a month and they were suffocating me. They had a UCC1 filing, which simply means everything I had was at their disposal. Other banks were not an option because it was during the Fannie Mae and Freddy Mac debacle and my financials sucked at the time. My supplier didn't want to hear about the $30 million in material I bought and paid for from them in the past. It didn't matter. They ended up writing off about a million bucks.

Well, I didn't quit, I started over. I would eventually negotiate a note on my home with the supplier and pay down debt through a Chapter 11 that would bring their $1,000,000.00 writeoff down to about $400k. The thing is: these are big boys, and they take risks every day when they extend credit. I am not making excuses at all, and I truly do still feel bad about it (just a little), but I am amazed how the dumbasses let me get up to over a million bucks anyway.

Now, here is the other side of the coin. Yes, they took a hit, and they actually wrote it off early so the $600k they would collect at a later point went right to their bottom line as profit. And as far as the remaining $400k they took a hit on, I have bought about another seven to eight million from them in materials. I didn't quit; I started over and because of it I came out better. Some of the people I hurt came out better in the long run, too.

- Finally, Gables said the last ingredient to winning championships is a hard-to-find alloy called guts. This means fighting through your fears, worries, and anxieties, and then moving on to the next one, and then moving on to the next one. Fear can motivate sometimes, but for the most part it freezes people. It's the old fight or flight syndrome and most people choose flight over fight. They run and hide.

Not a Kickassopotamus; they fight. They understand that there is no courage without fear and that fear masks itself in protection, but it is really nothing more than shackles. Let me repeat that one more time: fear masks itself in protection, but it is nothing more than shackles. Sometimes you have to stand up and be willing to go where no one has gone before. Take risks that are scary. The truth is the bigger the risk, the greater the reward.

Better Done Than Perfect

(Just like this book)

What many see as risky and dangerous behavior is one of the things that makes the Kickassopotamus so amazing. While everyone else in the world is dotting every "i" and crossing every "t" before they make a decision, the Kickassopotamus decides on a move and takes action. While others plan and spend countless hours before making a move, the Kickassopotamus gets three steps ahead. Of course it's wise to get as much information as possible and to take time to analyze good data, but most people never take action. The graveyard is full of the greatest ideas that have never came to fruition simply because people didn't move on them.

Being wise is part of the evolution process; however, sometimes you have to run through a wall just to get there first.

The other thing a lot of people do is they have to make everything perfect before rolling out the next best thing. I personally do not understand this philosophy at all.

I love my Harley Davidson Street Glide (they have been around for years) and I have a newer model. Harley hit a home run when they brought the bike to market. Was it perfect? Well, in my opinion it was pretty damn nice, but let me tell you about my 2016 model. It has an amazing sound system with Bluetooth technology (I love thumping *Back in Black* by AC/DC when I head down the road). It has an awesome navigation screen that allows me to travel anywhere day or night. It has a lot more cc's in the motor than the older models, and it really gets up and going pretty quickly. Some bikers hate this, but it has got ABS brakes. These are a real game-changer and even if some guys are too nostalgic or just plain old bullheaded to admit it, these brakes will save your life.

The point is this: if you wait to do something until it is perfect, you're being foolish. No matter how perfect you think something is there is a 99.9% chance you will change it or improve it over time. The sooner you get it going the sooner you can make the change, hence the saying "Better done than perfect."

Consistency Equals Discipline

Discipline Equals Consistency

Consistency will almost always equal success. The thing you probably do not want to hear is, "It all starts with you."

Many, many, many times you are the biggest problem when it comes to consistency and discipline. You are the visionary looking into the horizon, picking and choosing where to go next or what product or project to take on that will yield the most return on time, money, and effort. In the meantime, the day-to-day projects, tasks, or targets get missed or set to the side for the time being. It is far from intentional, it's just that your time is too valuable to be wasted on mundane tasks, right? Wrong! Oftentimes business owners are great at developing processes or improving on them. The problem is that they set the process, they follow up on them for a brief time, and everything seems to be going great. They expect by some great miraculous wonder it will continue without their involvement. They come back a few months later to check on the process, or even worse they need important data from the process to find out it is not there. They get a response like, "Oh, I didn't know you still wanted us to do so anymore because you did not ask for it." Unfortunately, I have lived this myself a few times in life and it was really detrimental to the business.

Here is a real life example: I set a process in place that my accounting person would print and save the A/R report every day and secure it in a safe place. I did this in hopes that if we ever lost our accounting we would still have a record of who owed what to us on any given day (yes, we back up our books daily). If for some reason there was a catastrophic failure in our computer system, we would have our A/R at our fingertips.

Well, as luck would have it, our IT company closed out the year for us and did not back up our current data, and voila: everything was lost and could not be recovered (even a forensic computer company couldn't find the data). We had to rebuild a whole year's worth of accounting.

I know this is the extreme example, and a process or procedure for the close out could have prevented the whole situation. The point is: if we would have at least followed up with a, "Let me see a hard copy of the A/R report" on a daily or weekly basis, I would have had the most important part of the data needed to start rebuilding our accounting system. Instead, we had to go off of memory, and with there being no history from a bank statement to reconcile it would be a guess at best. I wonder what we wrote off just because of a lack of discipline.

The good news is that, having discipline and consistency is a skillset that can be developed over time. And, once you get the ball rolling, it becomes easier and easier. Consistency is the key to success; it's right up there with number one.

Don't Be A Sucker

You Think You Have A Great Culture? Think Again.

Everyone loves working for you, and you're a sucker.
Culture: It's not all about cotton candy, clouds, unicorns, and everyone being happy.

First off, let me start out by saying, yes: a happy culture is a more productive, team-oriented place than a culture of hostility and poor morale. So of course people need to know they are appreciated and it's important to create an environment that is fun and enjoyable. I mean, after all, who wants to spend 40% of their day in a miserable place?

Here is the problem: owners and managers get so caught up in creating the fluffy, happy environment they forget all about results.

I am going to be vulnerable here and tell you something about myself as a leader. In the past I would walk around and beat my chest and say how much all of my employees liked working for me. We even went to the extent of sending out a confidential survey and we scored very high in 20 different categories. I was so proud. After sharing and listening to some people in my mentor group, I was shocked at some of the results they had. In addition, even though they shared some of the same frustrations as we all do, they definitely were not struggling with the same things I was or to the extreme I was. I would set a process or system in place and find out in a month or two that it had fallen by the wayside. Yes, you could be the problem, but at some point we have to trust people and be able to delegate tasks, systems and procedures.

The next time you are thinking about or measuring your culture, consider a few questions. First, how's the bottom line? How healthy is the balance sheet? Are systems and processes followed and kept in place? Do people follow through regularly? How do the people on your team handle change? Are people running to their cars peeling rubber out of the parking lot when there is still work to be done or people to serve?

If the answer is not favorable to these questions, then sit down and take a breath because you're not going to like this: you're a sucker.

Sorry if that sounds harsh, but I have lived it. I know what it's like to give and give and give and get back so little or no effort in return. So my employees like me...big deal! Isn't that what dogs are for? (Unconditional love, I mean.)

Yes, I want my employees to like me; yes, I want people to enjoy working with me. Yes, I want respect from my employees and in turn I want to respect and love them.

We very intentionally make sure our employees feel appreciated.

Here are a few things we do throughout the year:

- My key managers and I cook breakfast for all of our employees the last Friday of every month. (I am the best omelet-maker around.)
- We schedule a killer crab feast in the summer.
- Our holiday party is incredible.
- I personally hand write a letter to every new employee when they start. We include a copy of Andy Andrews' *The Butterfly Effect*, and a gift card as well.

The most important thing we do is pour into them by coaching and mentoring them professionally and personally. So, yes, we want to love and appreciate our employees; however, that is not the end all and be all. There has to be successful results for a culture to be dynamic. Systems and processes have to be followed and managed with consistency; this will bring joy to people, knowing there is structure in the organization.

The point is: culture is about doing all the little things, as well as the big things in this book.

EXERCISE:

Think about your culture. Answer the following:

     a.   Are systems and processes followed on a regular basis?

     b.   Is your company results-focused?

     c.   Are your results near your set targets and expectations?

     d.   Are your employees happy?

     e.   Is it a fun and dynamic atmosphere?

Kickassopotamuses Are Like Pokémon

They Evolve

Whether you are a millennial, Generation Z, Generation X, or even a Baby Boomer, chances are you have heard of Pokémon. These crazy little creatures were created in Japan in 1995. It seemed every kid around had to have a Pokémon card collection. The cartoon creatures and monsters would battle each other on the TV and in the palms of kids' hands in card games and video games. The cool thing is Pokémon creatures did not just stay where they were in life. They evolved into bigger and stronger Pokémon as time passed and even developed new super powers ("abilities," to you real Pokémon aficionados).

I have good news for you: no one is born a Kickassopotamus. They evolve over time. Some evolve through academics, mentoring, and coaching from others; however, if you're like most of us, you evolve through heartaches, poor decisions, and many wrong turns. Remember, the one thing that's always in the DNA of a Kickassopotamus, whether they are partially or fully evolved, is that they do not have the ability to quit. Therefore, the thing that makes most people quit—pain—actually becomes a blessing to the Kickassopotamus. They are smart enough not to wallow in self-pity; thus, they self-evaluate and make changes in their lives that help them gain knowledge. Even more importantly, they gain wisdom.

The rate at which you decide to evolve is totally up to you. For years I thought I was the cat's meow (whatever the hell that means). I started out in construction and became a very intelligent young man. At 22, I was one of the youngest men, if not the youngest in my state, to receive a Master Electrician's License (I got a special exemption to take the test because I had three years of electricity in high school and four years at a trade school). I would go on to test in other states and pass with flying colors. I even taught electrical school in my early 20s. I was at the top and figured, well, I guess I'm a pretty smart guy. I'm definitely smarter than my boss, and if he can run a business I know I can do it even better.

Long story short, I fell flat on my ass for the first time. Thank God I didn't know how to quit.

Even after having some failure in my life, I really was still always ahead of the pack. I always had more money in my pocket than my friends, so it was kind of hard to be humble and do some real self-evaluation. This can really be dangerous. No matter how high you are or how successful you become, "You don't know what you don't know." I would have to get kicked in the ass again a few more times before I could smell the bullshit I was carrying around.

It was time to get real. Evolving is a choice and I decided to evolve into something so strong and so smart and so wise that I would look alien to others. I read everything I could get my hands on. I attended seminars and I spent endless hours learning accounting. I developed systems and processes that were amazing. I dabbled in real estate with some success and expanded into many other areas of business over time.

I joined a group called Vistage, and I highly recommend it. I would go into a room once a month with nine other business owners for an entire day. We had our own speaker for the morning sessions; mid-morning to late afternoon, we would roll up our sleeves and get down and dirty and do some real work. One of my favorite things would be when someone would get on the hot seat to discuss a current problem or situation they were having in their business. Everyone would be put on a timer and allowed to ask the person on the hot seat questions (all you could do is ask questions). At the end of the session, the person on the hot seat would report back the questions they heard, and then everyone would be put back on the timer (limited to one or two minutes) and simply say, "If I were you I would (apply whatever here)."

Afterwards, the person on hot seat would repeat back the recommendations they heard, and they would take the information they gleaned and then do whatever they thought was best for them and apply it. Two weeks later my Vistage chair would show up for a one-on-one and mentor me and kind of kick me in the ass and hold me accountable.

A side note about my Vistage group: I was the most un-academic in the group, as we had engineers with PHDs, pharmaceutical CEOs with PHDs, and most had at least an MBA. And then there was me, the kid who barely made it through high school. I held my own and amazed myself as to how much I would bring value and worth to the group, especially when it came to understanding KPIs, balance sheets, and income statements. I was really starting to get it—and then my particular group disbanded.

I will always value my time there, as I gained some awesome friends, but my particular group falling apart became a blessing. I thought I was at the top of my game. These people helped bring me to a level I never even knew existed. Subsequently, I would stumble into another group called SGI (Success Group International). The information I gained there was not groundbreaking, nor would it shake the foundations of the earth, but it did give me a whole different way of thinking about business. Again, I got a couple of mentors who poured into me (thanks Bill and Dave).

Then, by chance I saw this friend of mine on Facebook wearing this crazy-looking warrior mask. I called him and he explained to me that he joined CEO Warrior. Remember earlier when I said, "You don't know what you don't know"? The information, knowledge, and wisdom that Mike Agugliaro brings through his CEO Warrior Program is like nothing you could ever imagine. He comes off a little crazy, but that's a good thing because he isn't stuck in the rut of thinking like everyone else. He thinks outside the box and serves at an unprecedented level. I would label Mike a Kickassopotamus who is ahead of the pack. And yet, he will tell you himself that he has evolved as a business owner, father, husband, and coach over the years.

The point is this this: evolution does not happen through osmosis. It does not come naturally. Evolution into this new type of superbeing is not a birthright. It's not even a choice, it's a decision. It takes hard work, it takes effort, and it takes hours of looking intently into the mirror. My mentor feeds himself through mentors. He invests time and money to spend time with some of the greatest people in the world, such as Tony Robbins and marketing guru Joe Polish. Agugliaro is an amazing speaker and he will tell you it did not come naturally. He went out and got trained and mentored by Joe Williams, a former speaker on the Tony Robbins circuit who now has his own speaker boot camp.

If you ever have the opportunity to sit in a room with a bunch of Tony Robbins worshippers (for the record, Tony is not looking for worshippers, he just wants to serve people and change their lives) get ready to be awed at the conversations. These people who have invested their lives in the Robbins way are off the hook, and I mean that in a good way. The conversations, thoughts, and insights you hear from these people are at a level above and beyond the norm. And it's not that they worship Tony; it's just that they found something that works, and they apply it on a regular basis.

Consequently, even though evolving into a Kickassopotamus does not come naturally, it can happen. No matter where you are in your evolution process, find a coach and/or a mentor who can pour into you. Find a group that can bring you success. Take a college class that can make a difference in the way you use information, or that can help you write better. Take a speaking class or go to Joe Williams' speaker boot camp. Spend time at Robbins' events, and if Mike Agugliaro has room in his CEO Warrior program, by all means join it.

Of course, all these things cost money; however, it will be the greatest investment you ever made.

Don't Listen To The Idle Chatter Of Monkeys

People suck. Sorry, but it's the truth. They want to cast their own fears, worries, and anxieties on to you. Don't listen to them. Your gut is usually right and you're the one taking the risk, doing the work, and doing whatever it takes to win. Listening to the naysayers zaps your energy, time, and efforts. It really does hold you back and frustrate you. You don't have to get emotional about this when it happens. The truth is that monkeys just don't know any better. They hate that you are outside the cage living life to the fullest (even if it is super hard), so they fling their proverbial waste at you (to be clear—and I really want you to get this—they are throwing shit at you). This is because, even if the door was wide open, they would be afraid to step out of the cage and consider living another way.

The premise of this book is that the most successful people in the world evolve through hard work, perseverance, and working through fear, along with a ton of attributes that need honing and evolution. A Kickassopotamus has skin so thick that the words and actions of other people rolls off them like water off a duck's back. Developing thick skin may be one of the toughest evolutionary processes one has to go through to find success. It's hard to develop because you are working so hard to make changes happen and build things that bless yourself, your family, and people around you. We take it personally, especially when the negativity comes from those closest to us. Remember, you are you and no one else can live inside your mind. No one but you has your passion and drive to succeed. No one but you understands your purpose.

Back to the monkeys and their idle chatter. Remember, they live in fear, and some people are not only scared for themselves but they are scared for you as well. They love you and do not want to see you go through pain. What they do not understand is that not following your dreams and passion, not *living*, is more painful for you than facing or going through some type of temporary setback.

The evolution of developing thick skin is necessary for this simple reason: when you go down the Hurt Feelings Road or Angry Street, you forfeit your power. Think about it: what do you accomplish when you are angry, hurt, or frustrated? Ask yourself right now: what offends you? When you know you are right—and even if you weren't—you had the balls to go and try. It sounds easy to say, but don't allow things to offend you, because there really is no benefit.

I heard once that you should visualize your comebacks while you are still on top. This idea is powerful and the truth is that rehearsing a comeback may help you over a hump quickly in the future.

- Don't react when the negativity, words, or actions come your way. I know there is fight inside of you and it comes naturally, and that is one of the attributes that makes you successful. But just take time and get away from the situation before you react.

- Sit somewhere quietly and analyze what was said and whether it really has an effect on you; better yet, analyze whether choosing to allow it to affect you has any value.

- Consider where is it coming from. In other words: are they commenting out of fear, jealousy, or, sometimes, out of love? The point is this: it's not you, it's all on them. Don't allow other people's insecurities take your power away.

I am not a big revenge guy and usually don't see any value in it. Leave that up to God or karma or whatever you personally believe. However, remember: you are not a wimp. Donald Trump wrote something like, "Get even at all costs." I am not sure if that is good advice or not, but if someone physically tries to hurt you, your family or business, than by all means kick their freaking ass. Sue their asses, pay a lawyer, and file suit. They will shit themselves. Pay a few bucks and let some suit and tie fight your battle while you are out building, inventing, and creating things that make a change in the world.

Trust your gut; you know a good idea when you have one. Move on it and take action.

Take Care Of The P's In Your Life

Short stories and tales are nice tools to share your view on things, but sometimes you have to cut through all the bullshit and get right to the point. That is exactly what I intend to do here. Recognizing the things that have the power to move you along in life are essential to your success. For me, the 12 P's listed below are tools that I use to evolve and get better every day.

Permission

Plan

Persuasion

Passion

Problems

Promises

Purpose

Perseverance

People

Power

Persistence

Pleasure

Permission:

Give yourself permission to slay dragons, hunt the beast, and get better every day. Give yourself permission to be successful. Give yourself permission to live a life of abundance, joy, and happiness. This is tough for a lot of people because they are stuck in the past carrying around a bunch of baggage of past failures and hurts. It's time to move on and live. Give yourself permission to slay each day as it comes by recognizing your worth and value. You are the only one of you; no one else in this world has your DNA, your fingerprints, your gifts or talents. Quit believing the lies that you have been telling yourself for the past 20 years and recognize that you are unique and created with a special purpose. You are beautiful, you are amazing, and you are smart.

Passion:

Finding your passion in life is one of the most critical things you need to do in order to really start to live. This is the thing that excites you to get out of bed every morning (let me rephrase that: it's the *things* that make you jump out of bed every day). You may have to dig deep here and really get to know yourself, self-evaluate, and continually ask yourself what makes you happy. By this I mean, truly happy. Be careful to not mistake something like hiding on the golf course, hunting, or scrapbooking as a passion just because that thing brings you relief from pain. When the game is over, the pain and problems will still be there. I am talking about real excitement and passion. The sooner you find this in life the quicker things will come together for you. It will motivate and give you direction and purpose to your life. It took me 50 years to recognize that my passion was simple: it was to help people. That passion is the motivation and drive for writing this book; it is the passion that motivates me every day to get better and grow; it is the passion that motivates me at work to help me grow and become self-aware; it is the motivation that allows me to speak in front of large groups of people; it is the motivation that allows me to go live on Facebook unrehearsed and speak from my heart. Get the point? When you find your passion it will flow through to every aspect of your life. So if golf is truly your thing: by all means, let it drive and motivate you, but just be careful and recognize your true talents. If you are 30 years old and decide golf is your passion and you want to become a pro, it's probably not going to happen. I don't want to be the monkey throwing shit at you here, and I definitely do not want to be a negative force or killjoy. Just be realistic. Find something that you love in the game and let that drive you to get better every day.

Purpose:

A lot of CEOs get stuck on building core values, vision, and mission statements for their companies, and they forget all about building a purpose statement for themselves. Personally I don't like the term "mission statement"; I prefer "purpose statement" for my company and myself. It gives me clarity on why we do what we do and not the mission at hand. After you have found your passion, it is time to find your purpose. In other words, what are you going to do to make a difference in your life and other people's lives that fits your passion? Dig deep.

Example:
My passion is to help people.
My purpose is to stop the suffering, heal the hurting; together, we are creating a new and better you.

Keep it simple.

Power:

I have some great news for you. You are more powerful than you can even comprehend. You can do more and accomplish more than you ever thought possible. When you find your passion and purpose in life, there will be no stopping you. I have literally been up since 2:00 a.m. with thoughts banging around in my head. I had to get up and put these thoughts on paper. It's now 4:46 a.m., and I am going strong; the day is planned and scheduled all the way up until 10:00 p.m. tonight. I am not looking at the day as hard or with dread. I am full of excitement and looking forward to slaying dragons and kicking some ass. Because of knowing what my passion and purpose are, I have more power than you could imagine.

Plan:

What is your strategy to fulfill your purpose? What is your map to success? What is the target or destination you want to reach and how are you going to get there? What is the next action step and the next step and the next? Don't run in circles aimlessly. Have a plan and that will get you on your way. Remember: "better done than perfect." Build your plan and know that you can always change your map and go down another road if things are not working. And the map you follow should be one you draw yourself. Sure, there is wisdom in following models that work, but creating something unique to you will be fun; it's yours and no one else's.

Problems:

Eat your vegetables first.

Remember how you couldn't get up from the table until you finished your vegetables? Worst of all, you had to finish all of the peas on your plate. You couldn't even slip them to the dog because even he wouldn't eat them. So what did you do? You ate the yummy stuff and let the peas sit. You couldn't get up from the table until they were gone so you shifted and moved them around with your fork for a while. Finally, you would give in and start to eat them, but by then they were even worse. They had become cold and congealed. Oh, the horror!

Here's a thought: what if you would have eaten your peas first? What if you would have walked up to the table and just shoved them in quickly and gotten it over with? Sure, they still taste like shit, but they're not coagulated into jelly peas. Now you can enjoy the rest of the meal. Chances are you will get up from the table a lot sooner and get back to play time.

If you have a problem, go ahead and tackle it head-on. How many times do we put up with people who are underperforming or, even worse, their attitude sucks and they are bringing down the rest of the team? Either coach them up, or fire their sorry asses. As soon as you take care of the problem you will feel instant relief. Sticking your head in the sand or hoping things will get better on their own never works. Letting problems persist in your life will ruin your culture and will rob you of your passion. It will steal your purpose and render you powerless.

Perseverance:

Perseverance is a muscle: the more you use it the stronger it gets. Getting knocked down is part of the game, but getting back up is the thing that keeps you from losing. Remember, pain is temporary, but quitting is forever.

Persistence:

Do not mistake persistence for perseverance. They are both muscles that get stronger as you use them, but persistence is totally different. Persistence is not about getting back up; it's more about pushing forward when you get tired. It's about consistency of managing systems and processes on a regularly scheduled plan. It's about going the extra mile or doing the extra work. It's about taking care of the little things so the big things take care of themselves.

Persuasion:

Mastering the art of persuasion is key to driving people to improve and produce results that are key to your own success. Honing this skill is key; but the truth is, you have to get better yourself every day. You have to be genuine and live the message you are sharing. Be very careful not to mistake persuasion for manipulation. Manipulation will get some short-term results, but people will see through it quickly and be less likely to follow the lead of a big bullshitter on the next go-round.

Promises:

I learned early in life to not go around making too many promises. None of us can predict the future, and things change. Making promises hastily can cause catastrophic results and people will feel let down if you cannot come through on your word, even if you have the greatest intentions in the world. They'll deem you a liar and not trust you. Your word is a promise. People only hear what's in it for them, and if you set an expectation without qualifying it, it is deemed a promise. For that reason, I will have conversations like the following:

"Larry, I know your goals and aspirations, and I will help you do everything I can to reach them. Remember, Larry, this is not a promise, as none of us can predict the future, but if things work out the way we want them to you will reach your goals. Is that clear? Larry, I want to make sure I am clear here. Will you repeat back to me what you just heard me say?"

The promises you need to make and keep are the ones you make to yourself. How many New Year's resolutions are broken in the first month? Imagine if you would have kept to all those resolutions over time. Where would you be in your life right now? You owe it to yourself to keep your word to yourself and live the life you deserve.

People:

Surround yourself with people who will support you, motivate you, set expectations for you, and hold you accountable. Surround yourself with likeminded people, but ones who are playing at a higher level than you. This will be one of the greatest ways for you to grow. I know it's nearly impossible to be with these type of masterminds constantly. You will spend many hours with people who are not up to your game. That's okay—just make sure you spend your time to coach them up. If they are not coachable or motivated, move on. You cannot pour into people who do not want help. Also, remember the negative monkeys. Don't waste your valuable time trying to convince them of living another way. They live in fear and until they get sick of it, they won't come out of the cage and ask for help.

Pleasure:

We started out this chapter talking about giving yourself permission to live an abundant life. It is just as important to take pleasure in the process of your own evolution. Take joy and have some fun in your success as well. You put in the work and took the risk—now enjoy it! We tend to worry about looking cocky, so we hide our victories. Sorry, but that just sounds awful to me. Find a charity that is close to your heart and support them, but don't hide your accomplishments; if anything, be an inspiration to others. Enjoy the day, enjoy the work, and have fun.

Your Kryptonite: Overcoming The Shiny New Object

Plan, Focus, Finish

Kind of like how Superman is susceptible to Kryptonite, the Kickassopotamus does have a weakness of its own. Remember, it has a Ferrari brain constantly running at 180 mph. You would think at this great speed it would only allow itself to focus on the road ahead; however, that is not the case. It can catch something in its peripheral vision pretty easily, and before you know it, it forgets where it was headed and makes a hard right turn to chase the shiny new object. The problem is the last great idea gets boring or delegated to someone else without the drive or passion to see it through. This leads to frustration for business owners quite often. Until they can break this cycle and learn to stay on task until the fruits of their labor are won they may evolve; but their results will never reach full potential. When they learn to stay on the straightaway of the road they are on and still move at lightning speed, they produce results that freaking blow the roof off.

Plan, Focus, Finish

Going against the grain and learning to plan, focus, and finish is a real key to success. Sometimes it is absolutely necessary to run through walls and destroy a few things along the way just to get a head start. But the truth is planning your steps along the way makes good common sense. Planning costs, knowing what tools are needed, and even considering obstacles ahead of time can alleviate a lot of pain in the future. Even planning the night before helps bring focus. And being able to stay focused—not chasing that furry little bunny down the rabbit trail—will bring you closer and closer to your targets and goals on a consistent basis. Focusing allows you to finish. Sure, there is more than one thing in the queue at a time that needs attention or more than part of the business that generates income, but finishing is the final step to dreams coming true.

One thing I have found that helps fight my kryptonite is to make a simple list when crazy ideas come into my head, or when the shiny new shiny thing comes along. It can be as simple as this:

What's next, just not yet?
1. Bring a new product to market that brings water purification
2. Open a division to provide CEO mentoring
3. Write a book (ha-ha too late)

This has really helped me to remain focused on the projects at hand. I put the list on my wall. It is always there. I don't have to worry about losing the thought, and at any time I can either remove something from the list or begin to bring it fruition.

Strengths and Opportunities

Here I go again, kicking everything the MBA was taught through years of training, and throwing it out the window. It's not that I don't respect the academic, it's that I truly believe you have to think outside the box and view things from a different perspective. Through trial and error, I have found things that work and things that don't. I have completed several SWOT analyses and found them to have little value. I believe time could be better spent elsewhere. So when the consultant comes in and says, "We need to do a SWOT analysis for your business," be leery of them. Chances are they are working out of a textbook and will bring little value outside of that book.

S: What are your *Strengths?*

W: What are your *Weaknesses?*

O: What are your *Opportunities?*

T: What are your *Threats?*

On the surface it sounds like a great idea, right? The idea is to find your *strengths* and build on them, evaluate your *weaknesses* and turn them into strengths. You also need to determine what *opportunities* are available to you. And you need to uncover the t*hreats* your business is facing, and ascertain how to turn those threats into opportunities. It would be great if this type of analysis were a real game changer; however, the truth is that *most of the time,* it's a complete *waste of time.* Allow me to jumble the process a little.

Opportunities

When I say "a SWOT analysis sucks," or "accountants suck," don't throw out the proverbial baby with the bath water. There is always some type of value in analysis. It is always wise to look at any and all opportunities available.

But here's a secret: an opportunity is not always the shiny new thing or the next best thing coming to market you should be looking for. Look for the low-hanging fruit. For example, the fast-food chain Chick-Fil-A makes the most of every sale. Employees use simple questions such as "Would you like to make that a meal?" or "Would you like to make that a large drink?" and "Would you like a brownie with your meal?" They are not running out into the street, dodging traffic, trying to drag in new customers. They found a recipe for success that works. They offer great service and a great product. Of course, they still market to the masses. However, the customer that's already at the window doesn't have any acquisition cost. Every sale above and beyond the chicken sandwich is more profitable and drives more revenue.

Another example is the country-style restaurant chain Cracker Barrel. Although I am not personally a big fan of their fine dining experience, I will visit there on occasion with family or friends. Every time I walk in the door—no, actually, *before* I even get in the door—I get excited about their business model. You have to walk by rocking chairs and Adirondack chairs. And yes, they are for sale. Then you walk in and are held hostage for five or ten minutes in their little mini-store that sells knickknacks while you wait for your table. And, incredibly, no matter what time of day it is, there is always a wait. The items they sell are low cost but high profit. Well, then the meal is finished and it's time to pay up. They've got you again! You have to walk up to the register, and there sits the candy that you loved as a kid that you didn't even know still existed and you have to indulge in a Sky Bar, O-Henry, Mallo Cup, Mary Jane, Charleston Chew, and oh, don't forget the good old Zagnut! I mean, when in the world will we have the opportunity to find something so great that can bring back childhood memories? I don't take offense with their business model at all. I love it and try to learn from it.

Threats

I don't see as much value in studying what *threats* you or your company face. I agree some things make good common sense, such as making sure you build a strong balance sheet that shows a real stockpile of cash in the bank, just in case there is some catastrophic event that might take place in the future and revenue gets turned off for one reason or another. Obviously, having low cash reserves is a real threat. You don't need to a do a SWOT analysis to know that.

The problem with viewing threats is that we tend to focus on our competition. Allow me to rephrase that: a baby Kickassopotamus tends to focus on the competition. A mature Kickassopotamus recognizes that their only true competitor is him or herself. They don't get caught up in pricing wars or worrying about what the guy next door is doing. They serve people, they build value, they kick ass and always provide WOW service. In return, they get rewarded handsomely for it. One more thing: looking at *threats* tends to bring people down the worry trail and there is absolutely no value in worrying. (More on worry later.)

Weaknesses

There is some benefit in evaluating your *weaknesses* in order that you may grow. Personally (and I hope you don't mind my honesty here), I am not really sure where I stand on this. I really don't think it's possible to turn a weakness into a strength. On a personal level, I could never imagine myself as this administrative guru that makes sure all the i's are dotted and the t's are crossed (for the record, I love people with this talent. If it wasn't for their talents, I'd be up shit creek constantly). I don't see it happening for me for the long-term. I am sure if it came down to it and something was on the line I could do it at least for a while.

However, over the long-term, I just don't see it in my DNA. The reason I am cautious here is that I don't want to make this thought an absolute. The whole premise of this book is that we can evolve into great leaders and business owners; and that leadership can bleed into everything else in our lives, such as our relationships and health. So, maybe I could evolve into an admin guru (yuck, I don't even like the sound of that!).

Back to evaluating your weaknesses: you already know where you suck. Just don't do those things. Find someone else to do them. If it's a business service or product you are not good at, leave it the hell alone and let the next guy do it. It's kind of like when we talked about threats earlier: spending time and energy focusing on your threats is futile at best, and focusing on your weaknesses tends to just tear you down, leaving you feeling terrible at the end of the day.

Strengths

Finally, let's have some fun. What are you good at doing? What are your *strengths*? What can you or your business do better than anyone else around you? Find your strengths and harness them. Grow it or them, cultivate them, feed them, and then go kick some freaking ass. This is no exaggeration at all. I am welling up in tears because I find this so freeing and so powerful. *I want it for you.* Many people want to focus on the negative. Screw that. I want you to stop what you are doing right now and embrace your inner genius. When you work to your strengths, things come more easily, and the results are multiplied at a greater rate.

You are stronger and more powerful than you can imagine. Spend your time harnessing that power. I would like to share some words from Marianne Williamson. She writes:

It is our light, not our darkness, that most frightens us.

Our deepest fear is not that we are inadequate.

Our deepest fear is that we are powerful beyond measure.

It is our light, not our darkness, that most frightens us.

We ask ourselves, who am I to be brilliant, gorgeous, talented, fabulous?

Actually, who are you not to be?

You are a child of God.

Your playing small does not serve the world.

There's nothing enlightened about shrinking so that other people won't feel insecure around you.

We were born to make manifest the glory of God that is within us.

It's not just in some of us; it's in everyone.

And as we let our own light shine,
we unconsciously give other people
permission to do the same.

As we are liberated from our own fear,
our presence automatically liberates others.

1. What are you great at doing?

   _____

2. What else are you great at doing?

   _____

3. What else are you great at doing?

   _____

4. What else are you great at doing?

   _____

5. What else are you great at doing?

   _____

6. What are you a genius at?

   _____

7. What else are you a genius at?

   _____

8. What are you passionate about?

   _____

Get the point? Build it on that. If you found the above exercise hard to do, just go back to a time when you had some success, whether it was a day, a week, a month, a year, or a decade or two ago. What was it? Find it, search it out. Was it playing a sport? Was it a time you put in extra work? Was it slaying it in drama club? Was it in the classroom? Find it, harness it, and build on it, and then do it some more. Now you're going to have so much drive and passion you won't get tired anymore. It's going to be hard to contain you. Your spirit has been set free. You are *the man*, you are *the woman*, and you are a super hero. Embrace it.

The problem with a SWOT analysis is we end up spending so much of the time focusing on threats from the outside and our own weaknesses on the inside we tend to go negative and that leads to worry.

A Kickassopotamus does not spend valuable time in Worryville.

Earlier we talked about vision and seeing things that are not there. Imagine a time as a child when you were in the back yard playing Cops and Robbers, or Cowboys and Indians, or you just kicked it for a while with your Barbie or GI Joe. The point is this: you were having fun using your imagination. For whatever reason, when people grow up they tend to lose their imagination. Well, that's not exactly true either. They still have it, it's just that they just tend to misuse it. As a Kickassopotamus myself, I find this hard to understand because time and again I see people use their imaginations to see and imagine the worst possible outcomes. This is a terrible travesty; I can't imagine the pain and turmoil this must cause in one's own mind. Our imagination was not meant to destroy; it was meant to build things. Our imaginations were not meant to tear down; they were meant to invent things. Our imaginations were not meant to cause anxiety and worry; they were intended to build things up and bring people and places to greater heights.

The SWOT will also have you looking in the past, and it's hard to go forward while looking in the rear view mirror.

Sure, it's wise to learn from the past. It's also wise to not repeat the same mistake over and over. However, oftentimes people carry around their mistakes as some type of badge of honor. It's not a badge to be proud of at all. It's a symbol to the world that says, "Hey, I am a dumbass." When we carry our past failures around long enough, it becomes part of who we are, stifling our ability to be successful, lead, and make sound decisions.

Carrying around baggage from past failures, poor decisions, and mistakes is like carrying a bag of rocks around with you everywhere you go. Put down the bag and move on.

In doing a SWOT, I am concerned that when we go down the trail of "What are the threats?" we will turn to worry. We may waste time and resources on frivolous, non-essential "threats" that will never happen anyway. 99% of the worst-case scenarios you imagine never come to fruition. Quit wasting time and lighten your load.

Secret Soup Ingredients

Here in my home state of Maryland, we're surrounded by the Chesapeake Bay just about anywhere you go. People take pride in their crabs, in their Old Bay, Natty Bo's, crab cakes, Rock Fish, O's and Ravens. My wife makes the best cream of crab soup on this side of the Mississippi. Actually, she probably makes the best in the world. Being from Maryland and being considered the queen of cream of crab soup is considered quite the honor. She is too kind, and shares the recipe with friends and family all the time. You won't get that from me, but I will tell you this: there are only four ingredients, plus good quality backfin crab meat and a few spices. The simplest recipes are often delicious and always stand the test of time.

The secret sauce to success is simple as well:

- 3 parts passion
- 2 parts purpose
- And a whole lot of power

Finding your *passion* is crucial. What is it that floats your boat? What gets your motor running? Find those things and find something to do with them. For example, my passion for writing this book was simple: I wanted to share things that will help people grow, create, and build.

> What is your passion? What gets your motor running and up and our of be in the morning?
>
> _____
>
> _____
>
> _____

Build your *purpose* around your passion. In other words: what do you want to do with your passion? Evolution takes time.

> Why is this so important to you? Who will you affect? What will happen when you are working in your passion?
>
> _____
>
> _____
>
> _____

When you find your *power*, you won't get tired; you'll work at a level you never knew existed. The good news is that once you find your passion you will automatically find your power. For now, just plan, focus, and finish working on your purpose with consistency. It's just like bringing the cream of crab soup to a simmer until it's time to indulge in a taste that is out of this world. I attempted to write this book several times over three or four years. When I finally figured out what I was passionate about saying, the words came together over a two-week process. I was so driven I couldn't stop writing.

The Right People, The Right Team

We talked about how the simple things in life usually stand the test of time. Rock and roll from the 1970s is a great example. Bands like Led Zeppelin, Aerosmith, ZZ Top, the Rolling Stones, and Pink Floyd are just a few illustrations of groups of individuals who slayed it on a regular basis. Each band member complemented one another. The music was simple, rhythmic, and had great lyrics with great singers and instrumentalists. Each member was right for that band at a particular time and place; on stage they had to trust that each member would do their part to make a masterpiece each and every time they played. It was a real team effort. Today's music does not even compare, what with all the electronics that new artists rely on. Sometimes, when they're live, they simply fall on their asses.

Another example of something that has stood the test of time is one of my childhood heroes. I couldn't wait for Saturday morning to come around so I could watch his antics. He was simple but intelligent. Bugs Bunny is the freaking man. I am not sure if there is a Cartoon Hall of Fame, but I would put him at the top of the list for such an honor. Unlike most of us, Bugs had the ability to get by on his own.

My favorite episode of all time is when Bugs took on the Gas House Gorillas in a baseball game. Bugs would take over for the Tea Totalers line up. The announcer came on and said, "There is a slight change in the lineup: now playing catcher, Bugs Bunny, left field, Bugs Bunny, right field, Bugs Bunny, pitching, Bugs Bunny, third base, Bugs Bunny." Okay, you get the point. Bugs was amazing. He would deliver a pitch and before you knew it he was behind home plate delivering banter and cheering himself on at the mound. He struck out three batters in a row with a single pitch. He hit the cover off the ball, scoring a ton of runs, and would even take on the manager's role and win a key argument with an umpire. Bugs would come from behind and recover from a 42-run deficit.

With the score at 96 to 95 and a man on first with two outs, Bugs delivered a pitch that one of the Gorillas destroyed with a bat the size of a tree. The ball was crushed and quickly left the park. For the first time in the story, Bugs needed some help. He dashed out of the

I wish I could remember where I read this, but I love this quote: "Hire slow, fire fast, and don't get sued." Take your time and continually look for A-players. Cut the cord on C-players quickly— and as far as not getting sued goes, good luck with that. You are a Kickassopotamus and you're ready for any fight that comes along, but don't be naïve: manage risk whenever you can.

Why

Communication is the key to success and there is no substitute for it. It will empower and motivate.

Communication doesn't mean you are always talking and giving your opinion. You don't have to comment on every situation. You don't have to win every argument. You especially don't have to finish someone else's thought or sentences. I know it's cliché but adhering to the old saying "You were given two ears and one mouth for a reason" will reap rewards and take you and your team to new heights much quicker than you could imagine. Kickassopotamuses think faster, act faster, and come up with solutions much faster than the average bear. Hence, in the interest of saving time we tend to finish other people's thoughts and sentences, or we share our solutions without any consideration for their point of view. The problem with this is that people will tend to believe you really do not care about the input or solutions that they may bring to the table. In the long run, people will stop stepping up with solutions that, in the future, could bring value.

Two reasons in particular will cause them to shut down. First, frustration: it truly does set in over time from hearing the "same old, same old" in meetings, and having you dominate everything or improve every process or solution. This will serve only to take the wind out of their sails. Eventually they will simply say to themselves, "What's the sense of helping?" Second, they become lazy. After all, why put in extra effort if they can fall back on their fearless leader time and again?

The most important part of communicating is listening. We all know you are the HKIC (Head Kickassopotamus in Charge), so shut up for a change and listen! Let people finish. To be on the safe side, when you think someone is done speaking, count to five or ten before you start talking. And by "talking," I don't mean "giving your input."

Here's a secret: if you want to wow people, take notes when they are talking and then repeat back all the key points you heard. Knowing that you are taking the time to listen will get their motors running and get them excited. It will also allow them to take ownership of projects. If you are going to grow, you can't do everything yourself.

You have to allow your team to grow. Taking notes and listening may actually allow *you* to learn something as well. If we do all the talking and have to give input on every situation we will never grow beyond our own capabilities.

Think about this: what if you never took the training wheels off your kid's bicycle? Would they ever learn to ride safely on their own? Probably not! This works the same way with your team. I know, I know, you already thought about how to improve on what they just brought to the table. So, wait a day or a week, and *then* bring them the idea. By listening to and investing in your people, you will learn what floats their boats. In time, you will be able to lead them to the idea you had without cramming it down their throats. Remember: there is a line between being persuasive and manipulative (refer back to the Ps). Be sure to lead only through persuasiveness.

There will be plenty of time for you to share your thoughts and to command action. After all, you are the one setting the vision and, more importantly, the targets. You are sailing the ship and it's important to know when to turn away from icebergs. Then you'll need to shout, "All hands on deck! Steer hard to starboard, steer hard to starboard!" And when the wind is at your back and the seas are calm, you can command, "Set the main sails."

As a business owner, one of the most important things you need to do is to move your team to clarity and deliver the *why*. Before you even start to deliver your thoughts or messages, examine whether the *why* is important to you as well. This self-reflection will most likely keep you focused and on the right track.

Answer these questions in front of your team:

> Why is this important?
>
> How will it improve our process?
>
> How will it make us better?
>
> How will it benefit our clients and customers?
>
> How will it improve our sales?
>
> How will it improve our bottom line?

Not only is it important to deliver why a project is important *to the company*, it is just as important to deliver why it is important *to the individual*.

I will share with you two of the things that I have learned about marketing that are the absolute most important to know.

First, people are not buying the service or product you are selling. They are buying what the product or service your are selling *does for them*. For this reason I don't spend time talking about myself or how great our company is. I let them know what benefits and rewards they will receive by using our services.

Second—and this goes right along with the first—always think in the sense of WIIFM: What's In It For Me? By "me" I mean your consumer, customer, or client. All they care about is how is it going to benefit them. They don't care if you are "Family owned and operated for over fifty years." They *do* care if you will make their life convenient. They care if your product will bring them joy or comfort. They don't care if your employees are drug tested, but knowing their homes and family will be safe when using your services because you administer drug tests tells a different story. Get the point?

Your employee is just as important as your client, and I would argue probably more important than any individual customer as a whole. Employees are there day in and day out, serving your team and fighting to build and grow your business. So, in addition to the questions above it's important to bring clarity and deliver the *why* to them as individuals. They really want to know WIIFM. Yes, sometimes it's simply a paycheck; but remember that if the why is not strong enough, chances are that there is less motivation to buy what you are selling. And in this case, what you are selling is what you are asking them to do).

As you deliver projects and delegate tasks, ask yourself these questions. They will bring clarity and deliver motivation to get the ball rolling:

What's in it for them?

How will this project benefit them?

Will this project bring them opportunities in the future?

Will this new system make their life easier in the long run?

Will it bring them financial benefits? (Be careful not to make promises you can't keep.)

Most importantly, will it make their job secure?

Be sure to bring clarity on these questions as well:

What is the desired outcome?

What is the target or expectation?

How will you measure its success?

When will you have accountability meetings?

(Refer to the recipe for success for the above questions.)

Upward Communication

Who needs sleep, anyway? Contrary to what a lot of people believe or say, you do need some downtime. I am not saying you need eight hours sleep a night, or even six. Everyone is wired differently and their body decides what they need. Waking up at 2:00 a.m. with your head swirling with thoughts is a common thing for business owners. It's waking up night after night that becomes a problem. I have heard many people say, "Oh, that's when you are being creative." You will get advice such as, "put a pen a paper next to your bed and jot down your ideas and you'll be able to go right back to sleep." Sorry, but that is total bullshit most of the time. We already know your mind runs at 180 mph nonstop and this is the time for you to recharge and refuel. Waking up in the middle of the night can be the equivalent of driving right by the gas station with an empty tank.

Yes, you may have a great idea come to you in the middle of the night. By all means, speak the idea into your fancy smartphone, and then go back to sleep if you can. Chances are you won't, because the shiny new object bouncing around in your head will make you too excited. Do what you need to do in this situation. Get up and write a plan, or put it on a to-do list of sorts. Unfortunately, it's usually not the great idea that wakes you up in the middle of the night. The thing that wakes you most often is wondering if delegated tasks, expectations, or targets you have set are being worked on. You understand why things you ask of people are so important and wondering whether those targets, tasks or expectations makes you restless.

I read a nice little book one time by Larry G. Linne called *Make the Noise Go Away*. The premise of the book was the power of an effective second-in-command. It talked about the communication between the owner and his second-in-command. The thing I got out of it most was the concept of upward communication.

What I mean is this: imagine a world where you set targets, delegate tasks, set expectations, or you put in place a system to manage processes and your direct reports keep you in the loop on a constant basis.

Here's an example:

> "Hey, boss, I know your expectation is that I will take a few minutes every morning and analyze A/R. We have no concerns at this time and everything looks great. I'll update you again in two days."

Wow, what a relief. This is one less thing that will wake you up in the middle of the night. The sleep won't come back right away because trust will have to be earned and established through regular bouts of upward communication.

Developing this concept in your culture is a real game-changer. You will have little success if you and your second-in-command do not have great communication.

Another example:

> "I know you set our target this month for $800k in sales; I understand it is the middle of the month, but I just wanted to give you a heads-up that when you look at the income statement, it appears as though we are only at 35% of our target. However, we have a lot of work in progress and expect billings to be very good over the next two weeks. Furthermore, we will meet or exceed your targets. I'll give you another update next Monday morning."

Or:

> "I know you set our target this month for $800k in sales; I understand it is the middle of the month, but I just want to give you a heads up that when you look at the income statement it appears as though we are only at 35% of our target. It looks like we are not going to hit our targets. With your permission, I will reduce labor by cutting overtime and cut the hours even further if possible in order that we may

still be profitable. I'll give you another update next Monday morning."

Make sure your people are comfortable delivering bad news. The bad can be fixed, but ignorance of the bad can be catastrophic. In the second example above, our second-in-command delivered a solution along with the problem. Train and coach your people to bring you solutions to problems. What if, when they brought bad news, a problem, or just maybe a new idea to the table, they brought the negatives along with the solutions?

As Kickassopotamuses, we train ourselves to look for the faults in other people's ideas or solutions. What if they did it for us? What if, after they gave us the four or five possible negatives for each solution and then said "I picked solution C because it has the least risk and the fewest obstacles and will most likely give us the greatest return on investment"? Wow, what the hell are you even doing in the building at this point? (just kidding, don't ever underestimate your value—although it might be fun to take some time for yourself once in a while!)

Imagine a world where not only was there upward communication between you and direct reports, but one where the people under your direct reports used upward communication with their managers. This world would not only let you sleep, but more importantly, would allow you to let your creative juices flow as you chart the course you and your team are on.

Wow, I might not go to sleep now. I might go into a coma or something.

Communicate, communicate, and communicate. Deliver the *why*. Empower through communication—and, oh: don't forget to shut the hell up and listen, listen, listen.

Evolve Or Die

The day we stop growing in our physical bodies is the day we start to die. The day a business becomes stagnant is the day it draws closer to an end. The evolution process should never stop. The day it stops is the day you are out to pasture. I can't imagine how cruel retirement must be, and I hope to keep evolving through the years myself.

Keep evolving. You're worth it and you owe it to yourself.

A Punch In The Face

I am truly honored that you took your time and worked your way through this book. I'm sure you are on your way and you will evolve into the greatest Kickassopotamus of all time.

However, if you are looking for a gold star because you finished reading a few things that I have written, you're up Crap Creek without a paddle. Also, if you found you gained motivation and inspiration through these writings, I would say BFD to that as well. Motivation and inspiration will only last so long and will almost always lead to exasperation. To evolve, you have to take massive action; you have to apply the things that fit for you. Knowledge is not power—applied knowledge is power. If you do nothing from this point forward you have simply become a consumer who chose entertainment over evolution.

Go to work and kick some ass.

Here Comes Rex

Earlier I mentioned that until I found my purpose and passion I found it almost impossible to get my thoughts on paper. This was a blessing for sure. The truth is I wasn't ready and I am grateful for the timing. This is because I feel the content is much better and stronger than it would have been a year or two ago.

The End.

Wait a minute—the end? What kind of bullshit is that? There is no end; there is only evolution, right?

I know there are plenty of things to share and improve on in the future. But remember how I said, "Better done than perfect"? Well, that's this book.

Just like Pokémon, I am sure this book will evolve from Kickassopotamus into Kickassopotamus Rex!

Be sure to go to Kickassopotamus.com, where you can write yourself a quick little bio and post your pic, to share with all your friends and family that you are an official Kickassopotamus.

I am Talbot Watkins,

I am a Child of God,

I am Patty's husband and I love her deeply,

I am Matthew and Nick's dad and they are the apple of my eye,

And I am your friend.

Peace out. Catch you on the flip. Love ya!

Recommended Reading List

Most people just read books without ever really applying what they've read. That said, if you choose to read any of the books that have helped me evolve, make sure you read them and then apply the sage advice within them.

- *7 Habits of Highly Effective People* by Steven Covey
- *The One Minute Manager* by Ken Blanchard
- *How to Win Friends and Influence People* by Dale Carnegie

- *Good to Great* by Jim Collins
- *Great by Choice* by Jim Collins
- *Think Big and Kick Ass* by Donald Trump
- *The Art of the Deal* by Donald Trump
- *Win* by Frank Luntz
- *Profits aren't Everything They are the Only Thing* by George Cloutier
- *The Travelers Gift* by Andy Andrews
- *The Seven Decisions* by Andy Andrews
- *The Art of Getting Things Done* by David Allen
- *Who Moved My Cheese?* By Spencer Johnson
- *Think and Grow Rich* by Napoleon Hill
- *Make the Noise Go Away* by Larry Linne
- The Road Less Traveled by M. Scott Peck
- Unleash the Power Within (Audio) by Tony Robbins
- *Kickassopotamus* by Talbot Watkins III (Sorry, I couldn't resist)
- *The Bible* by God

Made in the USA
Middletown, DE
30 September 2017